Caring for My Pet

Ferret

**Lynn Hamilton
and Katie Gillespie**

MEDIA ENHANCED BOOKS

AV2 BY WEIGL

ADDED VALUE • AUDIO VISUAL

www.av2books.com

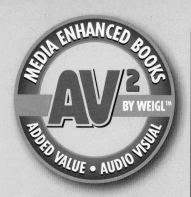

AV² provides enriched content that supplements and complements this book. Weigl's AV² books strive to create inspired learning and engage young minds in a total learning experience.

Your AV² Media Enhanced books come alive with...

Audio
Listen to sections of the book read aloud.

Key Words
Study vocabulary, and complete a matching word activity.

Video
Watch informative video clips.

Quizzes
Test your knowledge.

Go to **www.av2books.com**, and enter this book's unique code.

BOOK CODE

Z493774

Embedded Weblinks
Gain additional information for research.

Slide Show
View images and captions, and prepare a presentation.

AV² by Weigl brings you media enhanced books that support active learning.

Try This!
Complete activities and hands-on experiments.

... and much, much more!

Published by AV² by Weigl
350 5th Avenue, 59th Floor
New York, NY 10118
Websites: www.av2books.com www.weigl.com

Library of Congress Cataloging-in-Publication Data

Hamilton, Lynn, 1964- author.
[Ferret (AV2 by Weigl)]
Ferret / Lynn Hamilton and Katie Gillespie.
    pages cm. -- (Caring for my pet)
Includes index.
ISBN 978-1-4896-2954-8 (hard cover : alk. paper) -- ISBN 978-1-4896-2955-5 (soft cover : alk. paper) -- ISBN 978-1-4896-2956-2 (single user ebook) -- ISBN 978-1-4896-2957-9 (multi-user ebook)
1. Ferrets as pets--Juvenile literature. I. Gillespie, Katie, author. II. Title. III. Series: Caring for my pet.
SF459.F47H366 2016
636.976'628--dc23
                         2014041389

Printed in the United States of America in North Mankato, Minnesota
1 2 3 4 5 6 7 8 9 0 18 17 16 15 14

112014
WEP311214

Project Coordinator: Katie Gillespie
Designer: Mandy Christiansen

Ferret

Contents

Ferret Friends

Ferrets are playful, lively, and **mischievous** creatures. They like to chew, dig, tug, and bounce around. Some enjoy snuggling their owners or chasing other ferrets. These furry adventurers are often curious. They can find their way into small places, such as the sleeve of your coat.

Owning a ferret is a big responsibility. Your ferret will count on you to provide food and water. You will also need to keep her cage clean and supervise her while she is outside of her cage. You may want to train her to use a litter box, too. Pet owners need to make sure that their home is always a safe, happy, and healthy place.

Another name for ferret is "**fitchet**."

There are about **750,000** pet ferrets in the **United States.**

Ferrets are related to **badgers, skunks,** and **weasels**.

The **2 different species** of ferrets are the **common ferret** and the **black-footed ferret.**

Common ferrets are a tame form of the **European polecat**.

Ferrets may face many dangers in nature, such as predators, disease, lack of food, and extreme weather.

Ferret Firsts

No one knows for sure how long ferrets have been tamed and kept as pets. Some experts think that ferrets were first domesticated more than 2,500 years ago. The Egyptians may have been the first people to keep this animal.

It is important to make sure your area allows ferrets as pets. Check local game commission laws to see if a permit is needed to adopt a pet ferret.

Others believe that the Greeks were the first to domesticate ferrets. Records show that Romans used ferrets to chase rabbits from their burrows. These rabbits were caught for food. Over many centuries, this hunting method reached Great Britain and other European countries.

Ferrets were also used to catch and kill rodents during the 1870s in Spain. Some farmers thought that ferrets were pests, and hunters did not like having to compete with ferrets for **prey**. By the 1900s, chemicals were used to control rodent populations. As a result, it became illegal to own a ferret in several areas.

Today, ferrets have become popular pets, with **breeders** raising them to meet the growing demand. There are ferret clubs and organizations. People even show their pet ferrets in special competitions.

The ferret is a member of the **Mustelidae** family.

Ferrets were used **to catch rats** on ships sailing to the United States in the **15th century**.

Ferrets have a keen sense of **hearing** and an excellent sense of **smell**.

Ferrets breed easily in captivity. Female ferrets have an average of 12 to 14 babies, called kits, each year.

Pet Profile

Both male and female ferrets can make great pets. The most common pets are sable ferrets. Ferrets come in many patterns and colors. Some have patches on their knees, markings on their head, or white feet called mitts. A ferret's coloring does not affect his **temperament**. Each ferret is born with a unique personality. His behavior is influenced by the way his owner trains and treats him.

Sables

- Have dark brown **guard hairs**
- Have a white, cream, beige, or golden **undercoat**
- Are known for raccoon-like markings on the face
- Have a dark tail and legs
- Have black or brown eyes and nose
- May have a T-shaped pattern or speckles on the nose

Cinnamons

- Have reddish-brown guard hairs
- Have a white, beige, or golden undercoat
- Do not typically have heavy markings on the face
- Have burgundy eyes
- Have a pink, light brown, or reddish-brown nose
- May have a T-shaped pattern on the nose

Albinos

- Have white or cream guard hairs
- Have a white or cream undercoat
- Are lacking special dyes in the body, called pigments, which cause the coat to be white
- Have red eyes
- Have a pink nose
- Are also known as red-eyed white ferrets

Chocolates

- Have milk or chocolate brown guard hairs
- Have a white or golden undercoat
- Have brown or dark burgundy eyes
- Have a pink, beige, or reddish-brown nose
- May have a light brown, T-shaped pattern on the nose

Silver Mitts

- Have white guard hairs mixed with some darker strands
- Have a white or off-white undercoat
- Do not have as heavy markings on the face as other ferret varieties, such as the sable
- Have dark burgundy eyes
- Have white feet
- May have a white patch on the chest called a bib

Butterscotches

- Have butterscotch guard hairs
- Have a white, beige, or golden undercoat
- Are a lighter version of the sable ferret
- Have a darker tail, ears, and legs than the rest of the body, like most ferrets
- Have a butterscotch-colored nose
- Was once known as the Siamese ferret

Picking Your Pet

It is easy to see why ferrets have become such popular pets. These energetic animals are bright-eyed and cute. However, owning a ferret can be difficult. Think about the following questions before bringing home a pet ferret.

🐾 Ferrets are social animals that do best when raised together in small groups.

Can I Afford a Ferret?

Ferret prices will vary, depending on where you look. It may be less expensive to buy a ferret from a shelter than from a pet store or a breeder. Your pet ferret will need food and litter on a regular basis. She will also need a cage and some accessories. It will cost money to make sure your ferret stays healthy, too. Yearly check-ups, **vaccinations**, and getting your ferret **spayed** or **neutered** are all expenses to consider.

Will I Be a Responsible Owner?

In order to keep your ferret happy and healthy, you must keep a careful eye on her. She will depend on you for everything. You will have to make sure your home is safe for her to explore, under your supervision. Taking time to play with your ferret is also important. She will need time to exercise outside of her cage every day.

How Can I Make My Home Ferret-Friendly?

Everyday objects, such as pencil erasers, can be dangerous for your ferret, if eaten. Plants, electrical wiring, and household cleansers should also be moved out of her reach. Your pet ferret can crawl inside furniture, appliances, or furnace ducts. Any opening larger than 1 to 2 inches (2.5 to 5 centimeters) must be blocked. Ferrets can get along with cats and dogs, but they should not share a home with birds, fish, rodents, or snakes. Your ferret should be closely monitored at all times.

The **average** ferret costs between **$100** and **$150.**

Ferrets can grow up to **2 feet long.** (0.6 meters)

Baby ferrets can be adopted around **12 weeks** old.

Ferrets have **four different kinds** of teeth.

Neutered male ferrets are **more friendly** than those who have not been neutered.

Ferret toys should be made of hard plastic. Never give your ferret anything she can shred or tear.

Life Cycle

The average life span of a ferret is between 6 and 10 years. During this time, ferrets go through many changes. Knowing about the different stages of your ferret's life will help you to be a good pet owner. This will allow you to better understand and care for your pet ferret.

Newborn Ferrets

Newborn kits are born with their eyes closed. Their pink skin appears to be hairless, but they are actually covered with fine hairs. Kits are only about 2 inches (5 cm) long. A mother ferret usually gives birth to five or six kits at once. She is very protective of her kits and stays close by them.

First Weeks

Between three and four weeks of age, kits open their eyes and start eating soft food. They develop a thick, white coat as they mature. A kit's coat will darken over time, unless it is an albino. By five weeks old, kits' coats are thick and full. At six weeks, they are ready to be **weaned** from their mother's milk.

Senior Ferrets

As ferrets get older, they will need to sleep and snuggle with their owners more often. By age four, their fur might begin to turn white or gray and become thin. Senior ferrets' eyesight may start to fail, and they can develop arthritis or dental problems. More frequent trips to the **veterinarian** may be needed. Other issues can be dealt with at home. If a senior ferret's paw pads become dry, rubbing them with vitamin E cream or petroleum jelly can help keep them moist.

Adults

By six months, ferrets are fully grown. Adult males are called hobs. They grow up to 24 inches (61 cm) long and weigh between 3 and 5 pounds (1.4 and 2.3 kilograms). Adult females are called jills. They only grow to about 18 inches (46 cm), including their tail. Jills weigh between 1 and 3 pounds (0.5 and 1.4 kg). They are able to give birth within their first year.

Ferret Furnishings

There are a few key supplies you will need to take care of your pet ferret. These include ferret shampoo and claw clippers. If you plan to take your ferret outdoors for a walk, a leash and a harness will also be required. The most important things to get for your ferret are a cage and a litter box.

A wire cage works well because it has good **ventilation**. It makes a cozy home for your pet ferret, especially at night, or while you are away. Two ferrets can live comfortably in a cage with 2 to 3 foot (0.6 to 0.9 m) long sides. If you own more ferret friends, you will need a larger cage. It is important for the door of the cage to latch securely.

Your ferret will also need a litter box. It should be placed in the corner of the cage. Always keep your ferret's litter box, food, and sleeping areas separate.

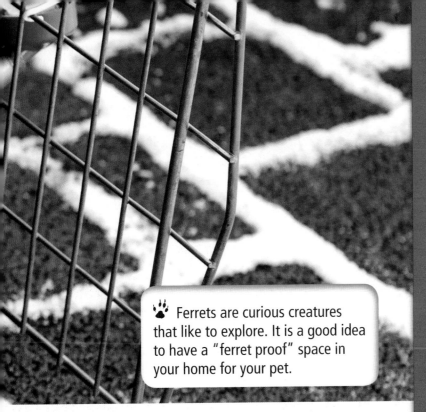

Ferrets are curious creatures that like to explore. It is a good idea to have a "ferret proof" space in your home for your pet.

Newborn ferrets are small enough to fit inside a **teaspoon**.

A ferret's tail is about **5 inches** long. (13 cm)

Ferrets have **five toes** on each **foot**.

Females have a thinner, more *pointed nose* than males.

The common ferret weighs **about 2 pounds.** (1 kilogram)

Male ferrets are **larger and heavier** than female ferrets.

The litter box should have sides measuring about 3 inches (8 cm) high, with one lower side, so that your ferret can easily go in and out. Putting a light layer of litter inside the litter box will keep your ferret from playing in it. Be careful what you use for litter, as some ferrets are **allergic** to wood chips and shavings. Paper, wood pellets, or dust-free litter are good options.

Ferrets need toys to play with as well. They love to tunnel, so tubes made from cut-off pant legs or dryer hoses are ferret favorites. These kinds of toys will keep your pet busy and interested. Make sure that you give your ferret toys made of **non-toxic** materials. They should not have loose or breakable parts, which could be swallowed by accident.

Feasts for Ferrets

Ferrets need to eat often, so their food bowls should never be empty. A constant supply of fresh water should also be available. When kits are being weaned, they need to have their food softened with water. Older ferrets can eat a variety of foods. Your ferret may be fussy about the kinds of foods he eats. Ask your ferret breeder or veterinarian for advice about the best brands of food.

There are special foods made just for ferrets. Some owners may feed their ferret a high-quality dry cat food instead of ferret food. However, soft cat food and dog food does not provide the proper nutrition for your ferret. Eating hard food helps keep your ferret's teeth clean. This is because **plaque** rubs off as he eats.

Feeding your ferret turkey or chicken bones is dangerous. Small pieces of bone may block your pet's intestines.

You can also feed your ferret bananas, raisins, and cooked chicken or beef as a treat. Avoid giving your ferret dairy products, nuts, chocolate, garlic, and onions. Ferrets have trouble digesting sugary foods. They digest their food too quickly to draw enough nutrients from vegetables. Too many fruits and vegetables may give your ferret diarrhea.

Your ferret's food must offer a good source of animal fat and animal protein. This will help him get the vitamins that he needs. Always check with your veterinarian to make sure that your ferret is receiving the right nutrition he needs to stay healthy.

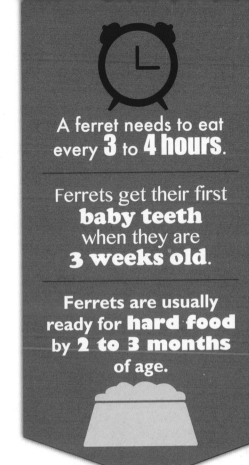

A ferret needs to eat every **3** to **4 hours**.

Ferrets get their first **baby teeth** when they are **3 weeks old**.

Ferrets are usually ready for **hard food** by **2 to 3 months** of age.

Ferrets have special teeth for tearing meat. These four long, sharp teeth are called canines.

Feet to Fur

Ferrets are very energetic animals. It is not surprising that such athletic creatures enjoy playing. Ferrets have very flexible bodies. They are also quite intelligent. Several features make ferrets exceptionally skilled at exploring and hunting.

Head

Ferrets have long heads that are flat on the top. This shape helps them run through very small spaces.

Eyes

Ferrets are best at viewing objects that are close. They can also see well in shadowy areas. Their eyes are placed slightly to the side and top of their head, which lets them see large areas.

Teeth

Ferrets get their permanent teeth between two and three months of age. As they get older, these teeth may start to yellow and become transparent.

Fur

A ferret's body is covered in thick, soft fur. She may shed in autumn, before growing a winter coat, and again in spring.

Legs

A ferret's short legs allow her to explore tight places. Their strength lets her climb, jump, and run. Ferrets use their claws for digging and grasping.

Tail

Ferrets have about eighteen bones in their tail. When she is scared or excited, the hair on a ferret's tail will stand on end. Excessive hair loss from the tail can be a sign of illness.

Scent Glands

A ferret has scent glands all over her body. These are what give her fur its musky scent.

Fluffing Ferrets

Ferrets groom themselves, but your pet will need some help from you. To control odors, clean your ferret's cage and change his bedding often. You should also clean your ferret's ears at least once each month. This can be done with a cotton swab and special ear cleansers. Do not try to clean inside the ear canal. This can damage your ferret's eardrum. Your pet ferret may also have tooth decay and cavities, just like a human. Your veterinarian can check and clean your ferret's teeth.

🐾 Running water may scare your pet ferret. You can help keep him calm by filling the bathtub before placing him inside.

You should clip your ferret's nails to help prevent them from getting caught in carpet or bedding. It is a good idea to ask an adult for help with this task. Be careful not to clip too far down, as this may cause bleeding or pain. There is a special powder available to stop the bleeding, in case you accidentally clip your ferret's claws too low.

If your ferret gets into something messy, he might need to have a bath. You can bathe your pet in a few inches of lukewarm water, using special ferret shampoo. Take care not to get soap in his eyes. When he is clean, rinse your ferret with warm water and dry him thoroughly. It is important not to bathe your ferret too often. Frequent baths will remove oils from his skin. Your ferret's body will try to replace these oils, which will result in a strong, musky smell.

Over time, you will become more familiar with your ferret's appearance and behavior. Watch for potential signs of illness, such as changes in appetite or bathroom habits. Other symptoms may include weight loss or gain, increased scratching, extreme sleepiness, and heavy hair loss or lumps. Many health problems can be prevented simply by giving your pet ferret plenty of exercise, proper nutrition, veterinary care, and a safe living environment.

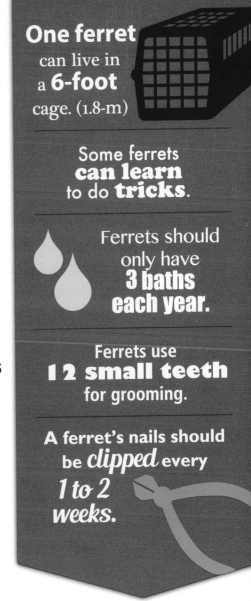

One ferret can live in a **6-foot** cage. (1.8-m)

Some ferrets **can learn** to do **tricks**.

Ferrets should only have **3 baths each year.**

Ferrets use **12 small teeth** for grooming.

A ferret's nails should be *clipped* every *1 to 2 weeks.*

Healthy and Happy

Ferrets can get hair balls, just like cats. These clumps of hair can be very dangerous. They may block your ferret's intestines. Your veterinarian can suggest a product to help prevent hair balls from forming. If your ferret has black, heavy ear wax, this may be a sign of **ear mites**. Ferrets can easily catch ear mites from other ferrets. There are special ear drops to help get rid of these pests. You can get them from your veterinarian.

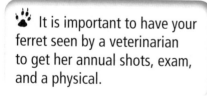
It is important to have your ferret seen by a veterinarian to get her annual shots, exam, and a physical.

Unlike most animals, ferrets can catch a cold or the flu from humans. Be careful to wash your hands before handling your pet ferret. If you are sick, do not cough or sneeze nearby. It is best to try to stay away from your ferret if you are ill.

Your ferret may also become sick in hot weather. Temperatures above 80 degrees Fahrenheit (27 degrees Celsius) can be bad for your pet. You may be able to tell if she is not feeling well by her behavior. If your ferret is limp or panting, she could be ill. Avoid problems by giving your ferret cool water or keeping her cool with a fan. Never leave your pet alone in a hot car.

Male and female ferrets should be **spayed or neutered** by 4 to 6 months of age.

 Ferrets should visit the vet **once a year.**

A ferret's diet should be made up of about **18 to 25% fat**.

Ferrets should have yearly **x-rays** and **blood tests** up to age 5.

A healthy ferret will eat **8 to 10 small meals** each day.

🐾 Like dogs, ferrets can catch fleas, but dog flea remedies can harm your ferret. Ask your vet how best to treat your pet.

Fun with Ferrets

Your pet will need time to adjust to his new home. Speak softly and approach him slowly at first. When you hold your ferret, always support his bottom. There are two ways to hold him. The first way is to grasp the loose skin at the back of his neck, called the scruff. The second way is to support his chest and front legs with one hand, while holding his behind with your other hand. This will make your ferret feel relaxed and safe.

An effective way to help prevent accidents is to place one or more litter boxes in the corners around your ferret's play area.

Just like a puppy, your ferret will need to be trained how to play nicely. You can teach him not to nip by picking him up by the scruff and firmly saying "no." Another way to discourage your ferret from biting is to spray a bitter apple flavor on your hands. He will not like the taste of the spray.

Ferrets are incredibly smart animals. They can be trained to use a litter box. To teach him, simply put your ferret in his litter box every half hour. Leave a bit of waste in the litter box to remind him of its purpose. Remember that if another area smells like his litter box, your pet will use it like one. If your ferret has an accident, clean the spot thoroughly.

Your pet ferret will also enjoy attention. He can be taught to roll over or sit up, and even to answer to his name. Chasing games or tug-of-war can be fun ways to spend time with your ferret. Use treats as a positive way to encourage good behavior.

Pet Peeves

Ferrets do not like:
- loud noises
- closed doors
- being held still
- dusty cat litter
- bitter apple flavor
- being too hot

ZZZZ ZZ
Ferrets **sleep** for 15 to 20 hours **each day**.

A ferret needs to play **outside** her cage for 4 to 6 hours **every day**.

Ferrets can **give off** an odor, like a **skunk**.

The name ferret comes from the Latin word *furonem*, which means "thief." Ferrets will often steal and hide household objects from their owners.

In the 1950s, ferrets were used to help catch rats in the London Underground.

Ferrets Forever

For thousands of years, ferrets have been helpful to humans. Specially trained ferrets have been used to pull cables through oil pipelines or string telephone wire underground. They wear small harnesses, attached to wires and cables, and tunnel to the other side where they receive tasty treats as a reward for their work. Today, ferrets are also used for medical research. They can help experts to study the flu or the effects of different medicines.

Ferrets are the subjects of websites, television shows, and movies. *Modern Ferret Magazine* is devoted especially to these interesting creatures. Author Richard Bach has even written a series of fiction books about ferret characters who have adventures and are involved in rescue missions.

Ferrets Tales

Ferrets are also the subject of some of Aesop's Fables. "The Snake, the House-Ferret, and the Mice" tells the tale of two mice who get caught in the middle of a fight between a snake and a ferret. While the ferret and the snake are fighting, the timid mice come out of hiding. When the ferret and the snake see the mice, they stop fighting each other and attack the mice instead. The moral of the story is that those who get involved in other people's fights may become victims of the fight.

Both **Queen Elizabeth I** and **Queen Victoria of England** owned ferrets.

The **black-footed** ferret is an **endangered** species.

Ferret breeding became so important in **New London, Ohio**, that the town became known as "*Ferretville.*"

Aesop's Fables were first printed more than 500 years ago. These stories are still popular today.

Pet Puzzlers

What do you know about ferrets? If you can answer the following questions correctly, you may be ready to own a pet ferret.

1. When can baby ferrets be adopted?

Around 12 weeks old

2. What color eyes does a silver mitt have?

Dark burgundy

3. How often does a ferret need to eat?

Every 3 to 4 hours

4. What kind of cage should you get for your ferret?

A wire cage

5. How long is the average life span of a ferret?

Between 6 and 10 years

6. What is an adult female ferret called?

A jill

7. What factors influence a ferret's behavior?

The way he is trained and treated by his owner

8. How many pet ferrets are there in the United States?

About 750,000

9. Why should you clip your ferret's nails?

To help prevent them from getting caught in carpet or bedding

10. At what age do ferrets get their permanent teeth?

Between two and three months old

Ferret Fame

Before you buy your pet ferret, write down some ferret names that you like. Some names may work better for a female ferret. Others may suit a male ferret. Here are just a few suggestions.

Felicity

Petunia

Chuckles

Cuddles

Columbus

Bandit

Digger

Franklin

Feisty

Key Words

allergic: to have a reaction to a substance

breeders: people who raise and sell animals

ear mites: small bugs that live inside an animal's ears

guard hairs: long, stiff hairs

mischievous: naughty

neutered: an operation that makes males unable to reproduce

non-toxic: not poisonous

plaque: sticky film on teeth

prey: animals that are hunted and eaten by other animals

spayed: an operation that makes females unable to reproduce

temperament: personality

undercoat: soft, fine, short hair

vaccinations: medicines given to help prevent diseases and illnesses

ventilation: clean, fresh air in an enclosed space

veterinarian: animal doctor

weaned: becoming used to food other than a mother's milk

Index

Log on to www.av2books.com

AV² by Weigl brings you media enhanced books that support active learning. Go to www.av2books.com, and enter the special code found on page 2 of this book. You will gain access to enriched and enhanced content that supplements and complements this book. Content includes video, audio, weblinks, quizzes, a slide show, and activities.

AV² Online Navigation

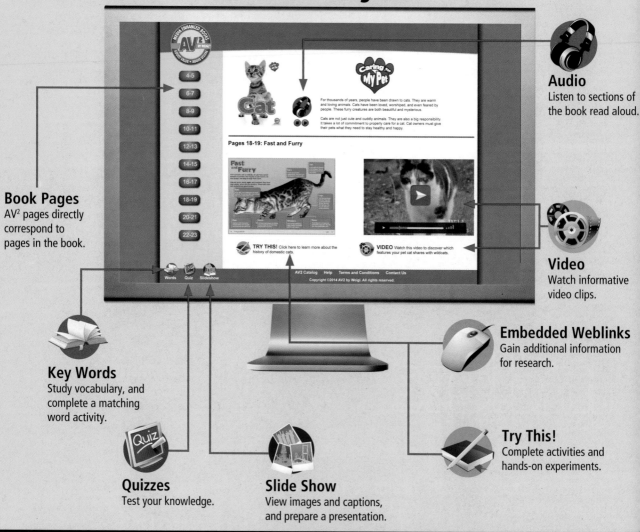

Audio
Listen to sections of the book read aloud.

Book Pages
AV² pages directly correspond to pages in the book.

Video
Watch informative video clips.

Key Words
Study vocabulary, and complete a matching word activity.

Embedded Weblinks
Gain additional information for research.

Quizzes
Test your knowledge.

Slide Show
View images and captions, and prepare a presentation.

Try This!
Complete activities and hands-on experiments.

AV² was built to bridge the gap between print and digital. We encourage you to tell us what you like and what you want to see in the future.

Sign up to be an AV² Ambassador at www.av2books.com/ambassador.

Due to the dynamic nature of the Internet, some of the URLs and activities provided as part of AV² by Weigl may have changed or ceased to exist. AV² by Weigl accepts no responsibility for any such changes. All media enhanced books are regularly monitored to update addresses and sites in a timely manner. Contact AV² by Weigl at 1-866-649-3445 or av2books@weigl.com with any questions, comments, or feedback.